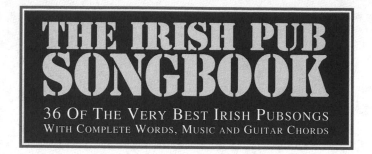

THE IRISH PUB SONGBOOK

36 OF THE VERY BEST IRISH PUBSONGS
WITH COMPLETE WORDS, MUSIC AND GUITAR CHORDS

D0376961

Ossian

Copyright 1993 © John Loesberg
Ossian Publications Ltd, Cork, Ireland
World Copyright, Made in Ireland

Design and lay-out by John Loesberg.
Typesetting by Grace O Halloran.
Cover Photograph by SlideFile, Dublin
Cover Artwork by Identity, Cork

'Rare Oul' Times' & 'The Fields of Athenry' © Pete St. John

Every effort has been made to ascertain the rights
on each song. The publishers beg to be informed of
any unintended infringements on any still existing rights.
Apart from the indicated copyright songs, all other
songs in this collection are copyright arrangements
by John Loesberg.
The editor thankfully acknowledges permission
given by publishers and composers of copyright material.

Printed at Watermans Printers, Cork, for
OSSIAN PUBLICATIONS,
PO BOX 84,
CORK, IRELAND

ISBN 0 946005 56 7
OMB 79

Contents

The Jug of Punch

'Twas ve - ry ear - ly in the month of June, as I was sit - ting
in my room I heard a thrush sing in a bush and the song it
sang was the jug of punch.___ Too - ra - loo - ra - loo, too - ra - loo - ra -
loo, too - ra - loo - ra - loo, too - ra - loo - ra - loo, I heard a thrush
sing in a bush and the song it sang was the Jug of Punch.___

What more diversion can a man desire,
Than to be seated by a snug coal fire,
Upon his knee a pretty wench
And on the table a jug of punch

If I were sick and very bad,
And was not able to go or stand,
I would not think it all amiss,
To pledge my shoes for a jug of punch.

The doctor fails with all his art,
To cure an impression on the heart,
But if life was gone, within an inch,
What would bring it back but a jug of punch.

But when I'm dead and in my grave,
No costly tombstone I will have,
But they'll dig a grave both wide and deep,
With a jug of punch at my head and feet.

OMB 79

Danny Boy

Oh, Dan-ny boy, the pipes, the pipes are cal-ling, From glen to glen and down the moun-tain - side, The sum-mer's gone and all the ro-ses fal - ling, 'Tis you 'tis you must go and I must bide, But come ye back when sum-mer's in the mea-dow, Or when the val - ley's hushed and white with snow. 'Tis I'll be there in sun - shine or in sha - dow, Oh Dan-ny boy, Oh Dan-ny boy I love you so.

And when you come and all the flowers are dying
If I am dead - as dead I well may be,
Ye'll come and find a place where I am lying,
And kneel and say an Ave there for me;
And I shall hear though soft your tread above me,
And all my grave shall warmer, sweeter be,
For you will bend and tell me that you love me,
And I shall live in peace until you come to me.

The Hills of Connemara

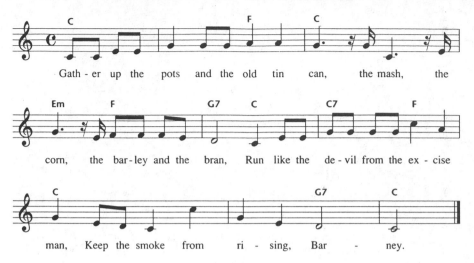

Gath - er up the pots and the old tin can, the mash, the corn, the bar-ley and the bran, Run like the de - vil from the ex - cise man, Keep the smoke from ri - sing, Bar - ney.

Keep your eyes well peeled today,
The tall, tall men are on their way,
Searching for the mountain tay,
In the Hills of Connemara.

Swing to the left and swing to the right,
The excise men will dance all night,
Drinking up the tay till the broad daylight,
In the Hills of Connemara.

A gallon for the butcher, a quart for Tom,
A bottle for poor old Father Tom,
To help the poor old dear along,
In the Hills of Connemara.

Stand your ground, it is too late,
The excise men are at the gate,
Glory be to Paddy, but they're drinking it nate,
In the Hills of Connemara.

OMB 79

The Black Velvet Band

As I went walk-ing down broad-way, not in-
A watch she pulled out of her pock-et and

ten-ding to stay ve-ry long I
slipped it right in-to my hand On the

met with a fro-lick-some dam-sel as she came a-trip-ping a-
ve-ry first day that I met her; bad luck to the black vel-vet

Chorus

long. Her eyes they shone like dia - you'd
band.

think she was queen of the land. With her hair thrown o-ver her

shoul-der tied up with a black vel-vet band.

'Twas in the town of Tralee an apprentice to trade I was bound,
With a-plenty of bright amusement to see the days go round.
Till misfortune and trouble came over me, which caused me to stray from my land,
Far away from my friends and relations, to follow the Black Velvet Band.

Before the judge and the jury the both of us had to appear,
And a gentleman swore to the jewellery - the case against us was clear,
For seven years transportation right unto Van Dieman's Land,
Far away from my friends and relations, to follow her Black Velvet Band.

Oh all you brave young Irish lads, a warning take by me,
Beware of the pretty young damsels that are knocking around in Tralee.
They'll treat you to whiskey and porter, until you're unable to stand,
And before you have time for to leave them, you are unto Van Dieman's Land.

I Never Will Marry

I ne-ver will mar - ry,____ I'll be no man's wife,____ I in-tend to stay sing - le,____ for the rest of my life.____

One day as I rambled down by the sea shore,
The wind it did whistle and the waters did roar.

I heard a poor maiden make a pitiful cry,
She sounded so lonesome at the waters nearby.

I never will marry, I'll be no man's wife,
I intend to stay single, for the rest of my life.

The shells in the ocean will be my deathbed,
And the fish in the water swim over my head.

My love's gone and left me, he's the one I adore,
I never will see him, no never, no more.

She plunged her fair body in the water so deep,
She closed her pretty blue eyes in the water to sleep.

I never will marry, I'll be no man's wife,
I intend to stay single, for the rest of my life.

OMB 79

The Rare Oul' Times

By Pete St John

Based on songs and sto - ries, he - roes of re - known.___ Are the
pas - sing tales and glo - ries, that once was Du - blin town. The
hal - lowed halls and hou - ses, the haunt - ing chil - dren's rhymes. That
once was part of Du - blin, in the rare_____ old times.

Chorus

Ring - a - ring - a - Ro - sie, as the light de - clines, I re-
mem - ber Du - blin ci - ty in the rare_____ oul' times.

My name it is Sean Dempsey, as Dublin as can be,
Born hard and late in Pimlico, in a house that ceased to be.
By trade I was a cooper, lost out to redundancy.
Like my house that fell to progress, my trade's a memory.
And I courted Peggy Dignan, as pretty as you please,
A rogue and child of Mary, from the rebel Liberties.
I lost her to a student chap, with skin as black as coal.
When he took her off to Birmingham, she took away my soul.
CHORUS

The years have made me bitter, the gargle dims my brain,
'Cause Dublin keeps on changing, and nothing seems the same.
The Pillar and the Met. have gone, the Royal long since pulled down,
As the great unyielding concrete, makes a city of my town.
CHORUS

Fare thee well, sweet Anna Liffey, I can no longer stay,
And watch the new glass cages, that spring up along the Quay.
My mind's too full of memories, too old to hear new chimes,
I'm part of what was Dublin, in the rare ould times.
CHORUS

THE CUSTOM HOUSE, DUBLIN.

OMB 79

A Bunch of Thyme

Come all you mai - dens young and fair,____ All you that are
bloom - ing in your prime____ And al - ways be - ware____ to
keep your gar - den fair, Let no man steal a - way your thyme.

For thyme it is a precious thing
And thyme brings all things to my mind
Thyme with all its flavours, along with all its joys,
Thyme brings all things to my mind.

Once I had a bunch of thyme
I thought it never would decay
Then came a lusty sailor, who chanced to pass my way,
And stole my bunch of thyme away.

Come all ye, etc.

The sailor gave to me a rose
A rose that never would decay
He gave it to me to keep me reminded
Of when he stole my thyme away.

Come all ye, etc.

Twenty-One Years

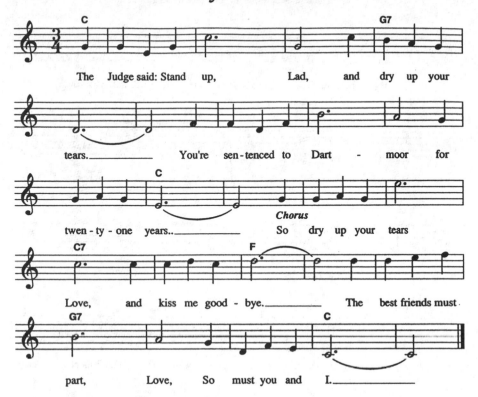

The Judge said: Stand up, Lad, and dry up your tears._____ You're sen-tenced to Dart - moor for twen-ty-one years.._____

Chorus

So dry up your tears Love, and kiss me good - bye._____ The best friends must part, Love, So must you and I._____

I hear the train coming, 'twill be here at nine.
To take me to Dartmoor to serve up my time.
I look down the railway and plainly I see,
You standing there waving your goodbyes to me.

Six months have gone by, love, I wish I were dead.
This dark dreary dungeon and stone for my bed.
It's hailing, it's raining, the moon gives no light.
Now won't you tell me, love, why you never write?

I've counted the days, love, I've counted the nights,
I've counted the footsteps, I've counted the lights,
I've counted the raindrops, I've counted the stars,
I've counted a million of these prison bars.

I've waited, I've trusted, I've longed for the day,
A lifetime, so lonely, now my hair's turning grey.
My thoughts are for you, love, till I'm out of my mind,
For twenty-one years is a mighty long time.

OMB 79

The Old Bog Road

By T. Brayton

My feet are here on Broad-way, this bles-sed har-vest morn. But

O, the ache that's in them for the spot where I was born. My

wea-ry hands are blist-ered from work in cold and heat. And

O, to swing a scythe to-day thro' fields of I-rish wheat. Had

I the chance to wan-der back, or own a king's a-bode. 'Tis

soon I'd see the haw-thorn tree by the Old Bog Road.

My mother died last springtime when Ireland's fields were green,
The neighbours said her waking was the finest ever seen;
There were snowdrops and primroses piled up beside her bed,
And Ferrans church was crowded when her funeral Mass was said.
But here was I on Broadway, and bitter was my load,
When they carried out her coffin down the Old Bog Road.

When I was young and innocent my mind was ill at ease,
Through dreaming of America and gold across the seas.
Och, sorra take their money - 'tis hard to get that same -
And what's the world to any man when no one speaks his name?
I've had my day, and here I am and bitter is my load,
A long three thousand miles away from the Old Bog Road.

There was a decent girl at home who used to walk with me,
Her eyes were soft and sorrowful like moonbeams on the sea;
Her name was Mary Dwyer - but that was long ago -
And the ways of God are wiser than the things a man may know;
She died the year I left her, and bitter was my load,
I'd best forget the times we met on the Old Bog Road.

Och, life's a weary puzzle, past finding out by man,
I take the day for what it's worth and do the best I can;
Since no one cares a rush for me, what need to make a moan,
I go my way and draw my pay and smoke my pipe alone,
Each human heart must know its grief, though little be its load,
So God be with old Ireland and the Old Bog Road.

Hotel at Maam.

OMB 79

The Old Triangle

A— hung - ry feel - ing, came o'er me steal— ing. And the mice were squeal - ing. In my pri - son cell.— — And that old tri - an - gle went jin - gle, jan— gle, All a - long the— banks of the Ro - yal Ca - nal——

To begin the morning, the warden's bawling:
'Get out of bed and clean up your cell'.
And that old triangle went jingle, jangle
Along the banks of the Royal Canal.

On a fine spring evening, the lag lay dreaming,
The seagulls wheeling high above the wall,
And the old triangle went jingle, jangle
Along the banks of the Royal Canal.

The screw was peeping, the lag was sleeping,
While he lay weeping for his girl Sal,
And the old triangle went jingle, jangle
Along the banks of the Royal Canal.

The wind was rising and the day declining,
As I lay pining in my prison cell,
And the old triangle went jingle, jangle
Along the banks of the Royal Canal.

In the female prison there are seventy women,
I wish it was with them that I did dwell,
Then that old triangle could jingle jangle
Along the banks of the Royal Canal.

The day was dying and the wind was sighing,
As I lay crying in my prison cell,
And the old triangle went jingle, jangle
Along the banks of the Royal Canal.

Galway Bay

By A. Cohalan

If you ever go across the sea to Ireland, Then may-be at the clos-ing of your day. You will sit and watch the moon rise o-ver Clad-dagh, And see the sun go down on Gal-way Bay.

Just to hear again the ripple of the trout stream,
The women in the meadows making hay,
And to sit beside a turf-fire in the cabin,
And to watch the barefoot Gossoons at their play.

For the breezes blowing o'er the seas from Ireland,
Are perfumed by the heather as they blow,
And the women in the uplands diggin' praties,
Speak a language that the strangers do not know.

For the strangers came and tried to teach us their way,
They scorn'd us just for being what we are,
But they might as well go chasing after moonbeams,
Or light a penny candle from a star.

And if there is going to be a life hereafter,
And somehow I am sure there's going to be,
I will ask God to let me make my heaven,
In that dear land across the Irish Sea.

OMB 79

Monto

Well if you've got a wing-o, take her up to Ring-o where the wax-ies sing o, all the day, If you've had your fill of por-ter and you can't go a-ny fur-ther, Give your man the or-der: Back to the Quay! And take her up to Mon-to, Mon-to, Mon-to, Take her up to Mon-to, lan-ge-roo, To you!

You've heard of the Duke of Gloucester, the dirty old imposter,
He got a mot and lost her, up the Furry Glen,
He first put on his bowler and he buttoned up his trousers,
And he whistled for a growler and he says, 'My man'
Take me up to etc.

You've heard of the Dublin Fusileers, the dirty old bamboozileers,
They went and got the childer, one, two, three.
Oh, marching from the Linen Hall there's one for every cannonball,
And Vick's going to send them all, o'er the sea.
But first go up to etc.

When Carey told on Skin-the-goat, O'Donnell caught him on the boat,
He wished he'd never been afloat, the filthy skite,
It wasn't very sensible to tell on the Invincibles,
They stood up for their principles, day and night.
And they all went up to etc.

18

Now when the Czar of Russia and the King of Prussia,
Landed in the Phoenix Park in a big balloon,
They asked the polismen to play 'The wearing of the green'
But the buggers in the depot didn't know the tune.
So they both went up to   etc.

Now the Queen she came to call on us, she wanted to see all of us,
I'm glad she didn't fall on us, she's eighteen stone.
'Mister Melord the Mayor', says she, 'Is this all you've got to show me?'
'Why, no ma'am, there's some more to see, póg mo thóin'
And he took her up to   etc.

HOWTH HARBOUR AND IRELAND'S EYE.

The Waxies' Dargle

Says my aul' wan to your aul' wan: Will yeh come to the Wax-ies dar-gle?' Says your aul' wan to my aul' wan: Sure I have-n't got a far-thing, I've just been down to Mon-to town to see un-cle Mc Ard-le, But he would-n't lend me half a crown for to go to the Wax-ies dar-gle, What are you ha-ving, will you have a pint, Yes, I'll have a pint with you Sir, And if one of ya does-n't or-der soon, we'll be thrown out of the boo-zer.

Chorus

Says my aul' wan to your aul' wan:
'Will you come to the Galway Races?'
Says your aul' wan to my aul' wan:
'With the price of my aul' lad's braces
I went down to Capel Street
To the Jew man moneylenders.
But they wouldn't give me a couple of bob on
My aul' lad's suspenders.'

Says my aul' wan to your aul' wan:
'We have no beef or mutton.
But if we go down to Monto town,
We might get a drink for nuttin'.
Here's a piece of advice
I from an aul' fishmonger
When food is scarce and you see the hearse
You'll know you have died of hunger.'

THE DARGLE.

GMB 79

The Rose of Tralee

The pale moon was ri-sing a-bove the green moun-tains, The sun was de-cli-ning be-neath the blue sea, When I stray'd with my love to the pure crys-tal foun-tain, That stands in the beau-ti-ful vale of Tra-lee. She was love-ly and fair as the rose of the sum-mer, Yet 'twas not her beau-ty a-lone that won me, Oh, no 'twas the truth in her eye e-ver daw-ning, That made me love Ma-ry, the Rose of Tra-lee.

The cool shades of evening their mantles were spreading,
And Mary, all smiles, sat listening to me,
The moon thro' the valley, her pale rays were shedding,
When I won the heart of the Rose of Tralee.
Tho' lovely and fair as the rose of the summer,
Yet 'twas not her beauty alone that won me,
Oh no, 'twas truth in her eye ever dawning,
That made me love Mary, the Rose of Tralee.

The Wild Rover

I've been a wild ro-ver for ma-ny's the year,_____ And I've
spent all me mo-ney on whis-key and beer,_____ And now I'm re-
tur-ning with gold in great store,_____ And I ne-ver will play the wild
ro-ver no more, *Chorus* And it's No, Nay, Ne-ver,_____
_____ No Nay Ne-ver No more,_____ Will I play_____
the wild ro-ver,_____ No, Ne-ver_____ No more.

I went to an alehouse I used to frequent,
And I told the landlady my money was spent.
I asked her for credit she answered me 'Nay,
Such custom as yours I could have every day.'
CHORUS

I brought up from my pockets ten sovereigns bright
And the landlady's eyes opened wide with delight.
She said 'I have whiskeys and wines of the best,
And the words that I told you were only in jest.'
CHORUS

I'll go home to my parents, confess what I've done,
And I'll ask them to pardon their prodigal son.
And when they've caressed me as oft times before,
I never will play the wild rover no more.
CHORUS

OMB 79

The Real Old Mountain Dew

Let gras-ses grow and wa-ters flow, In a free and ea-sy way. But

give me e-nough of the rare old stuff. That's made near Gal-way Bay, The

gau-gers all from Do-ne-gal, from Sli-go and Lei-trim too, Oh, we'll

give them the slip and we'll take a sip of the real old Moun-tain Dew. Hi the

Chorus

di-the-ry al the dal, dal the dal-the di-the-ry al, al the

dal dal di-the-ry-al dee - Hi the di-the-ry al the dal, dal the

dal the di-the-ry al, dal the dal dal di-the-ry al the dee.

24

At the foot of the hill there's a neat little still
Where the smoke curls up to the sky;
By a whiff of the smell you can plainly tell
That there's poitin, boys, close by.
CHORUS

For it fills the air with a perfume rare,
And betwixt both me and you,
As home we roll, we can drink a bowl,
Or a bucketful of mountain dew.
CHORUS

Now learned men who use the pen,
Have wrote the praises high
Of the sweet poitin from Ireland green
Distilled from wheat and rye.
CHORUS

Away with pills, it will cure all ills,
Of the Pagan, Christian or Jew;
So take off your coat and grease your throat
With the real old mountain dew.
CHORUS

Kate Kearney's Cottage.

OMB 79

Spancil Hill

Last night as I lay dream-ing of plea-sant days gone by, Me
mind bein' bent on ram-bling to Ire-land I did fly, I
stepped a-board a vi-sion and fol-lowed with my will, Till
next I came to an-chor at the cross near Span-cil Hill.___

Delighted by the novelty, enchanted with the scene,
Where in my early boyhood where often I had been.
I thought I heard a murmur and I think I hear it still,
It's the little stream of water that flows down Spancil Hill.

It being the twenty-third of June, the day before the fair,
When Ireland's sons and daughters in crowds assembled there.
The young, the old, the brave and the bold, they came for sport and kill,
There were jovial conversations at the cross of Spancil Hill.

I went to see my neighbours, to hear what they might say,
The old ones were all dead and gone, the others turning grey.
I met with tailor Quigley, he's as bold as ever still,
Sure he used to make my britches when I lived in Spancil Hill.

I paid a flying visit to my first and only love,
She's white as any lily and gentle as a dove.
She threw her arms around me, saying 'Johnny, I love you still'
She's Mag, the farmer's daughter and the pride of Spancil Hill.

I dreamt I stooped and kissed her as in the days of yore,
She said 'Johnny, you're only joking, as many's the time before.'
The cock crew in the morning, he crew both loud and shrill,
And I woke in California, many miles from Spancil Hill.

An Irish Interior, Showing a Hand Loom Weaver and a Spinner.

27

The German Clockwinder

A Ger-man clock-win-der to Dub-lin once came. Ben-ja-min Fooks was the old Ger-man's name, And as he was wind-ing his way round the strand He played on his flute and the mu-sic was grand. Sing-ing: Too-ra-lum-a-lum-a, Toor-a-lum-a-lum-a toor-a-de-ay. Toor-a-de, Toor-a-de, Toor-a-de ay, Toor-a-lum-a-lum-a, Toor-a-lum-a-lum-a. Toor-a-de-ay. Toor-a-de. Your-a-de-Your-a-de-ay.

Oh there was a young lady from Grosvenor Square
Who said that her clock was in need of repair
In walks the bould German and to her delight
In less than five minutes he had her clock right.
CHORUS

Now as they were seated down on the floor
There came this very loud knock on the door
In walked her husband and great was his shock
For to see the ould German wind up his wife's clock.
CHORUS

The husband says he, 'Now look here Mary Anne
Don't let that bould German come in here again
He wound up your clock and left mine on the shelf
If your oul' clock needs winding, sure I'll wind it meself.'
CHORUS

THOMOND BRIDGE, LIMERICK.

29

Whiskey in the Jar

As I was go-ing o-ver, the Kil-ma-gen-ny moun-tain, I met with Cap-tain

Far-rell and his mo-ney he was coun-ting, I first pro-duced me pis-tol, and

then I drew my sa-bre, say-ing 'Stand and de-li-ver for I am a bold de-

Chorus

cei-ver. With me ring dum a doo-dle um dah, whack fol the

dad-dy o, whack fol the dad-dy o, there's whis-key in the jar.

He counted out his money and it made a pretty penny,
I put it in my pocket and I gave it to my Jenny.
She sighed and she swore that she never would betray me
But the devil take the women for they never can be easy
CHORUS

I went into my chamber all for to take a slumber
I dreamt of gold and jewels and for sure it was no wonder
But Jenny drew my charges and she filled them up with water
And she sent for Captain Farrell to be ready for the slaughter
CHORUS

And 'twas early in the morning before I rose to travel
Up comes a band of footmen and likewise Captain Farrell;
I then produced my pistol, for she stole my sabre,
But I couldn't shoot the water, so a prisoner I was taken.
CHORUS

And if anyone can aid me, its my brother in the army
If I could learn his station in Cork or in Killarney,
And if he'd come and join me, we'd go roving in Kilkenny
I'll engage he'll treat me fairer than my darling sporting Jenny.
CHORUS

DROGHEDA FROM THE RAILWAY BRIDGE.

OMB 79

Quare Bungle Rye

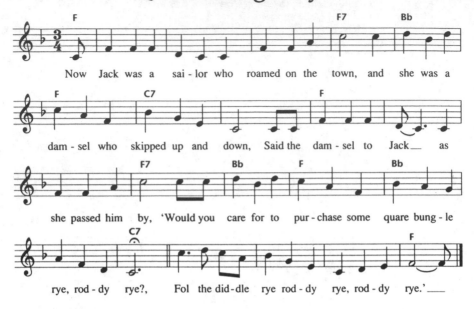

Now Jack was a sai-lor who roamed on the town, and she was a
dam-sel who skipped up and down, Said the dam-sel to Jack___ as
she passed him by, 'Would you care for to pur-chase some quare bung-le
rye, rod-dy rye?, Fol the did-dle rye rod-dy rye, rod-dy rye.'___

Thought Jack to himself 'Now what can this be,
But the finest of whiskey from far Germany,
Smuggled up in a basket and sold on the sly,
And the name that it goes by is quare bungle rye, roddy rye,' etc.

Jack gave her a pound and he thought nothing strange,
Said she 'Hold the basket till I get you your change.'
Jack looked in the basket and a baby did spy,
'Oh Begorrah,' says Jack, 'This is a quare bungle rye, roddy rye,' etc.

Now to get the child christened was Jack's first intent,
For to get the child christened to the parson he went.
Says the parson to Jack, 'What will he go by?'
'Bedad, now,' says Jack, 'Call him quare bungle rye, roddy rye,' etc.

Says the parson to Jack, 'Now that's a queer name,'
Says Jack to the parson, 'It's a queer way he came,
Smuggled up in a basket and sold on the sly,
And the name that he'll go by is Quare Bungle Rye, Roddy Rye,' etc.

Now all you young sailors who roam on the town,
Beware of those damsels who skip up and down,
Take a look in their baskets as they pass you by,
Or else they might sell you some quare bungle rye, roddy rye, etc.

Grafton Street—Bank on left—College on right.

Johnny Jump Up

I'll tell you a sto-ry that hap-pened to me one
day as I went down to Youghal by the sea. The
sun it was bright and the day it was warm. So, says
I, a quiet pint would-n't do me no harm.

I went in and I called for a bottle of stout:
Says the barman 'I'm sorry, all the beer is sold out,
Try whiskey or Paddy, ten years in the wood.'
Says I 'I'll try cider, I heard it was good.'

O never, O never, O never again,
If I live to a hundred or a hundred and ten,
For I fell to the ground and I couldn't get up
After drinking a quart of the Johnny Jump Up.

After lowering the third I made straight for the yard,
Where I bumped into Brophy, the big Civic Guard.
'Come here to me boy, don't you know I'm the law?'
Well I up with me fist and I shattered his jaw.

He fell to the ground with his knees doubled up
But it wasn't I hit him, 'twas Johnny Jump Up.
The next thing I met down in Youghal by the sea
Was a cripple on crutches and says he to me:

'I'm afraid of me life I'll be hit by a car
Won't you help me across to the the Railwayman's Bar?'
After drinking a quart of the cider so sweet
He threw down his crutches and danced on his feet

I went up the Lee Road, a friend for to see,
They call it the madhouse in Cork by the Lee.
But when I got up there the truth I do tell
They had the poor so-and-so tied up in a cell.

Said a guard testing him 'Say these words if you can:
"Around the rugged rocks the ragged rascal ran" '
Tell them I'm not crazy, tell them I'm not mad -
It was only a sup of the bottle I had.

A man died in the Union, by the name of McNabb.
We washed him and laid him outside on a slab,
And after O'Connor his measurements did take
His wife took him home to a bloody fine wake

'Twas about twelve o'clock and the beer it was high:
The corpse he jumped up and says he with a sigh:
'I can't get to heaven, they won't let me up
Till I bring them a quart of the Johnny-Jump-Up.'

Crosshaven.

OMB 79

Dicey Reilly

Ah, poor old Di - cey Ri - ley she has ta - ken to the sup, And

poor old Di - cey Ri - ley she will ne - ver give it up, It's

off each morn - ing to the pop and then she's in for an -

o - ther lit - tle drop, Ah, the heart of the rowl is Di - cey Ri - ley.

She walks down Fitzgibbon Street with an independent air,
And then it's down to Summerhill, at her the people stare,
She says 'It's nearly half past one,
So I'll nip in for another little one'
Ah, the heart of the rowl is Dicey Reilly.

She owns a little sweetshop at the corner of the street,
And every evening after school I go to wash her feet,
She leaves me there to mind the shop,
While she nips in for another little drop,
Ah, the heart of the rowl is Dicey Reilly.

I'm a Rover and Seldom Sober

I'm a ro - ver and sel - dom so - ber, I'm a ro - ver of high de - gree,____ It's when I'm drink - ing I'm al - ways think - ing how to gain my love's com - pa - ny.____

Though the night be as dark as dungeon,
Not a star to be seen above,
I will be guided without a stumble,
Into the arms of my own true love.

He stepped up to her bedroom window,
Kneeling gently upon a stone,
He rapped at her bedroom window,
'Darling dear, do you lie alone?'

It's only me your own true lover,
Open the door and let me in,
For I have come on a long journey
And I'm near drenched to the skin.

She opened the door with the greatest pleasure,
She opened the door and she let him in
They both shook hands and embraced each other,
Until the morning they lay as one.

The cocks were crawing, the birds were whistling,
The steams they ran free about the brae,
'Remember lass, I'm a ploughman laddie,
And the farmer I must obey.'

Now my love, I must go and leave thee
And though the hills they are high above,
I will climb them with greater pleasure,
Since I've been in the arms of my love.

OMB 79

Will You Go, Lassie, Go?

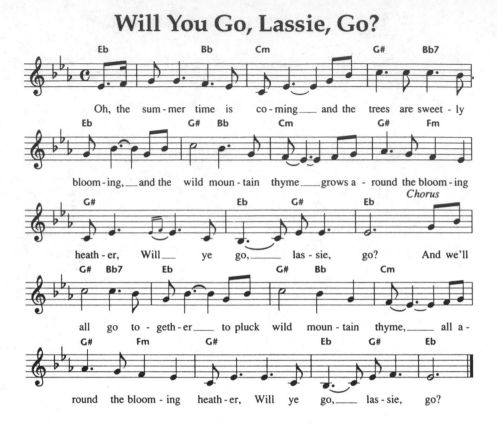

Oh, the summer time is coming and the trees are sweetly blooming, and the wild mountain thyme grows around the blooming heather, Will ye go, lassie, go? And we'll all go together to pluck wild mountain thyme, all around the blooming heather, Will ye go, lassie, go?

I will build my love a tower near yon pure crystal fountain,
And on it I will pile all the flowers of the mountain,
Will ye go, lassie, go?
CHORUS

If my true love she were gone, I would surely find another,
Where wild mountain thyme grows around the blooming heather,
Will ye go, lassie, go?
CHORUS

All for me Grog

Well it's all for me grog, me jol-ly jol-ly grog, It's all for me beer and to-bac-co, For I spent all me tin on the las-sies drink-ing gin, far a-cross the wes-tern o-cean I must wan-der.

Where are me boots, me noggin', noggin' boots,
They're all gone for beer and tobacco.
For the heels they are worn out and the toes are kicked about,
And the soles are looking out for better weather.

Where is me shirt, me noggin', noggin' shirt,
It's all gone for beer and tobacco,
For the collar is all worn, and the sleeves they are all torn,
And the tail is looking out for better weather.

I'm sick in the head and I haven't been to bed,
Since I first came ashore from me slumber,
For I spent all me dough on the lassies don't you know,
Far across the Western Ocean I must wander.

OMB 79

Finnegan's Wake

Tim Fin-ne-gan lived in Wat-ling street, a gent-le-man I-rish, migh-ty odd, He had a tongue both rich and sweet and to rise in the world he car-ried a hod, Now Tim had a sort of a tip-ling way, with a love of the li-quor poor Tim was born and to help him on his way each day, he'd a drop of the cra-tur e-v'ry morn Whack fol de da now dance to your part-ner, 'round the floor yer trot-ters shake, Was-n't it the truth I told you; Lots of fun at Fin-ne-gan's wake.

One morning Tim was rather full
His head felt heavy which made him shake
He fell from the ladder and broke his skull
So they carried him home, his corpse to wake.
They wrapped him up in a nice clean sheet
And laid him out upon the bed
With a gallon of whiskey at his feet
And a barrel of porter at his head.
CHORUS

His friends assembled at the wake
And Mrs Finnegan called for lunch
First they brought in tay and cakes
Then pipes, tobacco and whiskey punch.
Miss Biddy O'Brien began to cry
'Such a neat clean corpse did you ever see
Yerrah Tim, avourneen, why did you die?'
'Ah hold your tongue', says Paddy Magee.
CHORUS

Then Biddy O'Connor took up the moan
'Biddy' says she, 'you're wrong I'm sure'
But Biddy gave her a belt in the gob
And left her sprawling on the floor.
Oh then a mighty war did rage
'Twas woman to woman and man to man
Shillelagh law did all engage
And a row and ruction soon began.
CHORUS

Then Mickey Maloney ducked his head
When a naggin of whiskey flew at him
It missed him, falling on the bed
The liquor splattered over Tim.
Bedad, he revives and see how he rises
And Timothy rising from the bed
Says 'Fling your whiskey round like blazes
Thunderin' Jaysus, do you think I'm dead?'
CHORUS

OMB 79

Mother Machree

By Young/Olcott

There's a spot in me heart which no col - leen may own. There's a
depth in me soul nev - er sound - ed or known. There's a
place in my mem' - ry, my life that you fill. No oth - er can take it, no
one ev - er will. Sure I love the dear sil - ver that shines in your
hair. And the brow that's all fur - rowed, and wrin - kled with care. I
kiss the dear fin - gers, so toil - worn for me. Oh, God
bless you and keep you, Moth - er Ma - chree.____

Every sorrow or care in the dear days gone by,
Was made bright by the light of the smile in your eye;
Like a candle that's set in a window at night,
Your fond love has cheered me and guided me right.
CHORUS

DONEGAL CASTLE.

Do You Want Your Old Lobby

I've a nice lit - tle cot and a small bit of land and a place by the side of the sea._____ And I care a - bout no - one, be - cause I be - lieve there's no - bo - dy cares a - bout me._____ My peace is des - troyed and I'm fair - ly an - noyed, by a las - sie who works in the town. She sighs ev' - ry day as she pas - ses the way: 'Do you want your old lob - by washed down?'_____

Chorus

_____ 'Do you want your old lob - by washed down, Con Shine, Do you want your old lob - by washed down?' She sighs ev' - ry day as she pas - ses the way: 'Do you want your old lob - by washed down?'

The other day the old landlord came by for his rent
I told him no money I had,
Besides 'twasn't fair to ask me to pay,
The times were so awfully bad.
He felt discontent at not getting his rent,
And he shook his big head in a frown,
Says he 'I'll take half'. 'But', says I with a laugh
'Do you want your old lobby washed down?'
CHORUS

Now the boys look so bashful when they go out courtin'
They seem to look so very shy,
As to kiss a young maid, sure they seem half afraid,
But they would if they could on the sly.
But me I do things in a different way,
I don't give a nod or a frown.
When I goes to court I says 'Here goes for sport,
Do you want your old lobby washed down?'
CHORUS

Street in Galway.

OMB 79

The Fields of Athenry

By Pete St John

By the lone - ly pri - son wall._____ I heard a young girl call - - ing

Mi-chael, they are ta - king you a - way,_____ For you stole Tre-vel-yn's corn. So the young might see__ the morn. Now a

pri - son ship lies wait-ing in the bay._____

Chorus Low, lie the Fields_____ of A-then - ry, where once we watched the small free birds fly._____ Our__

love was on the wing, We had dreams and songs to sing. It's so lone - ly 'round the fields of A-then - ry._____

By a lonely prison wall
I heard a young man calling,
Nothing matters Mary when you're free,
Against the Famine and the Crown,
I rebelled they ran me down,
Now you must raise our child with dignity.
CHORUS

By a lonely harbour wall
She watched the last star falling
And that prison ship sailed out against the sky.
Sure she'll wait and hope and pray
For her love in Botany Bay,
It's so lonely round the fields of Athenry.
CHORUS

A CONNAUGHT CABIN.

OMB 79

The Stone Outside Dan Murphy's Door

By J.P. Dane

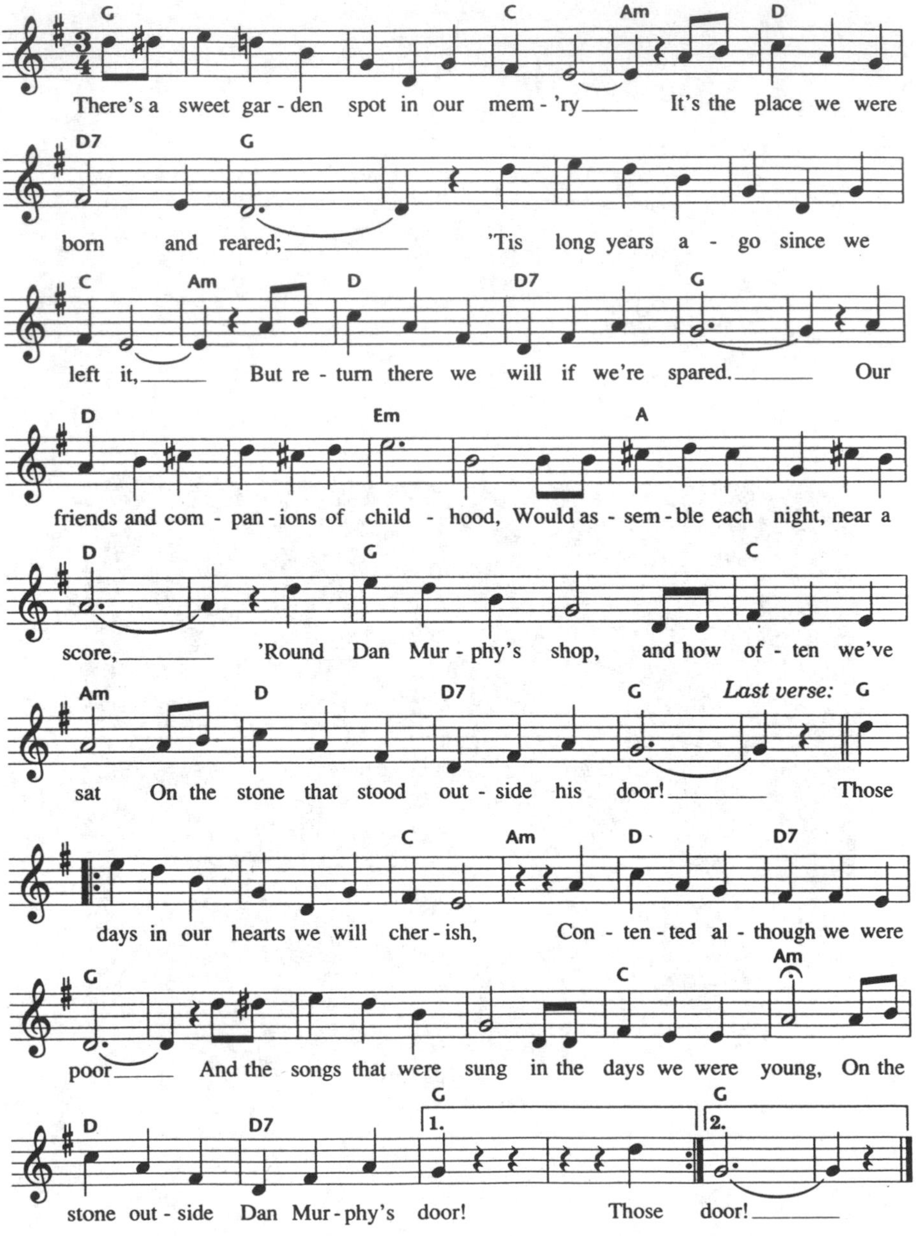

G C Am D
There's a sweet gar - den spot in our mem - 'ry It's the place we were
D7 G
born and reared; 'Tis long years a - go since we
C Am D D7 G
left it, But re - turn there we will if we're spared. Our
D Em A
friends and com - pan - ions of child - hood, Would as - sem - ble each night, near a
D G C
score, 'Round Dan Mur - phy's shop, and how of - ten we've
Am D D7 G Last verse: G
sat On the stone that stood out - side his door! Those
C Am D D7
days in our hearts we will cher - ish, Con - ten - ted al - though we were
G C Am
poor And the songs that were sung in the days we were young, On the
D D7 G 1. G 2.
stone out - side Dan Mur - phy's door! Those door!

When our day's work was over we'd meet there,
In the winter or spring the same,
The boys and the girls all together
Then would join in some innocent game.
Dan Murphy would bring down his fiddle,
While his daughters looked after the store,
The music would ring and sweet songs we would sing
On the stone outside Dan Murphy's door.

Back again will our thoughts often wander,
To the scene of our childhood's home,
The friends and companions we left there.
It was poverty caused us to roam.
Since then in this life we have prospered,
But now still in our hearts we feel sure,
For mem'ry will fly to the days now gone by
And the stone outside Dan Murphy's door.

(Last verse)
Those days in our hearts we will cherish,
Contented although we were poor,
And the songs that were sung in the days we were young,
On the stone outside Dan Murphy's door!

City of Limerick.

OMB 79

The Leaving of Liverpool

Fare - well to Prin - ces' land - ing stage, ri - ver Mer - sey fare thee well,_____ I am bound for Ca - li - for - ni - ay, A place I know right well._____ So fare. thee well, my own true love when I re - turn u - ni - ted we will be, It's not the lea - ving of Li - ver - pool that grieves_____ me, but my dar - ling when I think of thee._____

I have shipped on a Yankee sailing ship,
Davy Crockett is her name,
And Burgess is the captain of her,
And they say that she's a floating shame.
CHORUS

Oh the sun is on the harbour love,
And I wish I could remain,
For I know it will be a long, long time,
Before I see you again.
CHORUS

The Cliffs of Dooneen

You may tra-vel far, far, from your own na-tive home, Far a-way o'er the moun-tains, far a-way o'er the foam, But of all the fine pla-ces that I've e-ver been, Oh, there's none___ can com-pare with the Cliffs of Doo-neen.___

It's a nice place to be on a fine summer's day,
Watching all the wild flowers that ne'er do decay,
Oh, the hare and the pheasant are plain to be seen,
Making homes for their young round the Cliffs of Dooneen.

Take a view o'er the mountains, fine sights you'll see there;
You'll see the high rocky mountains on the west coast of Clare,
Oh, the towns of Kilkee and Kilrush can be seen,
From the high rocky slopes round the Cliffs of Dooneen.

So fare thee well to Dooneen, fare thee well for a while,
And although we are parted by the raging sea wild,
Once again I will wander with my Irish colleen,
Round the high rocky slopes of the Cliffs of Dooneen.

51

OMB 79

Nora

The chestnut blooms gleamed through the glade, Nora,
A robin sang loud from a tree,
When I first said I loved only you, Nora,
And you said you loved only me.

The golden-robed daffodils shone, Nora,
And danced in the breeze on the lea,
When I first said I loved only you, Nora,
And you said you loved only me.

The trees, birds and bees sang a song, Nora,
Of happier transports to be,
When I first said I loved only you, Nora,
And you said you loved only me.

The Bog Down in the Valley-O

Chorus

O - ro the rat - lin' bog, the bog down in the val - ley - O,

O - ro the rat - tlin' bog, the bog down in the val - ley - O.

1. And in that bog there was a tree, a rare tree, a rat-tlin' tree, with a
2. Now on that tree there was a limb, a rare limb, a rat-tlin' limb, with a
3. Now on that limb there was a branch, a rare branch, a rat-tlin' branch, with a
4. Now on that branch there was a twig, a rare twig, a rat-tlin' twig, with a
5. Now on that twig there was a nest, a rare nest, a rat-tlin' nest, with a
6. Now in that nest there was a egg, a rare egg, a rat-tlin' egg, with a
7. Now on that egg there was a bird, a rare bird, a rat-tlin' bird, with a
8. Now on that bird there was a feather, a rare feather, a rat-tlin' feather, with a
9. Now on that feather there was a flea, a rare flea, a rat-tlin' flea, with a

First verse only

tree in the bog and the bog down in the val - ley - O.

Pick up the remainder of verse at the corresponding number, continue from there to finish. Sing Chorus between every verse.

flea on the fea-ther with the fea-ther on the bird with the bird in the egg with the

egg in the nest with the nest on the twig with the twig on the branch with the

branch on the limb with the limb on the tree with the tree in the bog,

with the bog down in the val - ley - O!

OMB 79

Dirty Old Town

By Ewan McColl

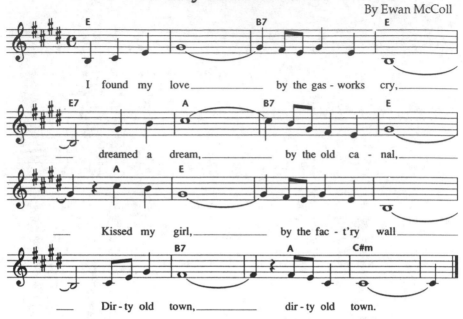

I found my love by the gas-works cry,
dreamed a dream, by the old ca-nal,
Kissed my girl, by the fac-t'ry wall
Dir-ty old town, dir-ty old town.

I heard a siren from the dock,
Saw a train set the night on fire,
Smelled the spring in the smoky wind,
Dirty old town, dirty old town.

Clouds are drifting across the moon,
Cats are prowling on their beat,
Spring's a girl in the street at night,
Dirty old town, dirty old town.

I'm going to make a good sharp axe,
Shining steel, tempered in the fire,
We'll chop you down like an old dead tree,
Dirty old town, dirty old town.

The Parting Glass

Oh, all the mo-ney e'er I had, I spent it in good com-pa-ny, And all the harm I've e-ver done, a-las it was to none but me, And all I've done for want of wit to mem'-ry now I can't re-call; So fill to me the part-ing glass, Good night and joy be with you all.

Oh, all the comrades e'er I had,
They're sorry for my going away,
And all the sweethearts e'er I had,
They'd wished me one more day to stay.
But since it falls unto my lot,
That I should rise and you should not,
I gently rise and softly call,
Goodnight and joy be with you all.

If I had money enough to spend,
And leisure time to sit awhile,
There is a fair maid in this town,
That sorely has my heart beguiled.
Her rosy cheeks and ruby lips,
I own, she has my heart in thrall,
Then fill to me the parting glass,
Goodnight and joy be with you all.

OMB 79

Publisher's Note :
The majority of songs included in this collection follow the same format of
our well-known *'Folksongs and Ballads Popular in Ireland'* by John Loesberg.
'Folksongs and Ballads' however features no less than 200 songs within the
four volumes available. Information on the origins of each song is also
included.

Folksongs and Ballads Popular in Ireland, Volume 1
collected, edited and arranged by John Loesberg
(OMB 1)
Folksongs and Ballads Popular in Ireland, Volume 2
(OMB 2)
Folksongs and Ballads Popular in Ireland, Volume 3
(OMB 3)
Folksongs and Ballads Popular in Ireland, Volume 4
(OMB 4)

Also in preparation is a large collection of Irish songs
'The Four Provinces Collection of Irish Songs and Ballad'
which will contain 250 songs from all parts of the country
and featuring many unusual traditional folksongs.
(Available Autumn 1993)

Ossian Publications produce a huge range of Irish Music,
ranging from Sheetmusic, Songbooks, Tune Collections,
Instruction Books to an acclaimed catalogue of
Traditional Irish Music on Cassette tapes and CD's.
For a complete list of all our publications please send your
name and address together with an (international)
Postal Reply Coupon to;

•**Ossian Publications Ltd.**•
P.O.Box 84, Cork, Ireland